Praise for *

Keeping Christ in Christmas is a challenge for every Christian family. Tracey shares some meaningful and very doable ways of keeping "the reason for the season" at the center of it all. This is a book you'll refer to again and again.

Terry Meeuwsen
Co-host, The 700 Club
Founder, Orphan's Promise

In a day when the world's focus has turned completely away from Jesus Christ, the only Savior of that same world, Tracey Moore's outstanding and much-needed book, ***Keeping Christ in Christmas***, will help parents and caregivers to teach their children the true meaning of Christmas in a way that will foster eternal results. I highly recommend this book by an author who is solidly grounded in the Word of God and whose writing and teaching you can always trust.

Dr. MaryAnn Diorio
Novelist and Life Coach

I loved believing in Santa and hyping him up for my children, too. I wanted Christmases to be magical. As the years passed, I realized just how little time I had spent (apart from midnight mass and shouting out an occasional "Happy birthday, Jesus!") actually focusing on the true reason for Christmas and the true Giver of the gifts. I felt guilty but had no idea what to do instead. I just knew that if I were able to go back in time, I would rethink my decisions about sharing the reality of Santa with my children and teach them instead about the true Gift-giver, Jesus. So when I picked up Ms. Moore's book with the intention of simply perusing it, I found myself reading every page, thinking the whole time, "Yes!! This is exactly what I would have done and what every believer should do!"

The book was not only well written, but Tracey clearly referenced the history of St. Nicholas and the tradition that developed because of him. She also referenced the Bible for every one of her thought-provoking options throughout the book. More importantly, she gave specific and actionable ideas parents can implement this Christmas and every Christmas thereafter.

Keeping Christ in Christmas is definitely a book I wish I'd had on my bookshelf thirty years ago. Though my children are now grown, I definitely plan to get this invaluable book into their hands so that together we can make Jesus the center of my grandchildren's Christmas. Thank you, Tracey, for this book! It is likely the best birthday gift Jesus could have ever hoped for.

Christine M. Bacon, Ph.D.
Author, *The Super Couple*
Radio Host, Breakfast with Bacon

KEEPING CHRIST IN CHRISTMAS

Thought-Provoking Ideas for
Making Jesus the Center of
Your Child's Christmas Holiday

Tracey L. Moore

Copyright © 2020 by Tracey L. Moore

All rights reserved. This book, or parts thereof, may not be reproduced in any form, stored in a retrieval system, or transmitted in any form by any means—electronic, mechanical, photocopy, recording, or otherwise—except for brief quotations in printed reviews, without the prior written permission of the author, except as provided by United States of America copyright law.

ISBN: 978-0-9891346-5-1

Unless otherwise noted, all Scripture quotations are taken from the New King James Version. Copyright © 1982 by Thomas Nelson, Inc. Used by permission. All rights reserved

Scripture quotations marked (NASB) are taken from the NEW AMERICAN STANDARD BIBLE, Copyright © 1960, 1962, 1963 1968, 1971, 1972, 1973 1975, 1977, 1995 by The Lockman Foundation. All rights reserved. Used by permission.
http://www.Lockman.org

Scripture quotations marked (NIV) are taken from the Holy Bible, New International Version®, NIV®. Copyright © 1973, 1978, 1984, 2011 by Biblica, Inc.™ Used by permission of Zondervan. All rights reserved worldwide (www.zondervan.com). The "NIV" and "New International Version" are trademarks registered in the United States Patent and Trademark Office by Biblica, Inc.™

All quotes from "The War on Christmas" by Dr. MaryAnn Diorio are used by permission of the author. The original post appears at https://maryanndiorio.com/2018/12/24/the-war-on-christmas.

Excerpt from *The Super Couple: A Formula for Extreme Happiness in Marriage* by Christine M. Bacon, Ph.D. Reprinted by Permission.

Cover Photo: Christmas Ornament (https://www.istockphoto.com)

Cover and book design by Tracey L. Moore

Edited by Janet Bagby

TABLE OF CONTENTS

ACKNOWLEDGMENTS vi
INTRODUCTION vii
CHAPTER 1
    WHO WAS ST. NICHOLAS, ANYWAY? 1
CHAPTER 2
    IS IT REALLY WORTH THE RISK? 13
CHAPTER 3
    CULTIVATING A MINDSET OF
    GIVING VS. GETTING 23
CHAPTER 4
    MAKING JESUS THE GIFT-GIVER 39
CHAPTER 5
    MAKING THE TRANSITION
    FROM SANTA TO JESUS 53
CHAPTER 6
    KEEPING CHRIST AT THE CENTER 65
CHAPTER 7
    'TWAS THE NIGHT BEFORE
    JESUS' BIRTHDAY 79
CONCLUSION 85
NOTES 89
ABOUT THE AUTHOR 95

ACKNOWLEDGMENTS

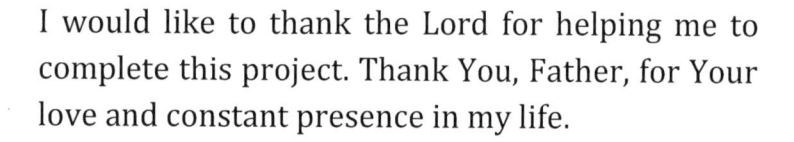

I would like to thank the Lord for helping me to complete this project. Thank You, Father, for Your love and constant presence in my life.

Thanks to my Lord and Savior, Jesus Christ, Who came to earth and was born to die for the sins of the world. Obviously, without Him, there would be no Christmas.

Thanks to my family and friends who encouraged and supported me in my publishing effort.

Thanks to Janet Bagby, who so graciously agreed to be my editor and has enhanced my work.

Thanks to you, the reader, for your desire to read what I have written. I do not take it lightly that you have decided to allow me to come into your world. I appreciate your support.

INTRODUCTION

One late November evening, as I sat in a Bible study at my church, someone asked the question, "Should we teach our kids to believe in Santa Claus or not?" A lively discussion ensued in which the group participants went around and around giving various opinions and trains of thought. After everyone had been given the chance to chime in, we concluded as a group that when it's all said and done, teaching kids to believe in Santa Claus takes the focus off Jesus and could wind up detracting from their spiritual growth in the end. Then a parent who had already taught her child to believe in Santa asked, "What do we do now?" That is a very good question.

I went home and went to bed thinking about what we had discussed that evening. One sister in the Bible study said she remembered as a child feeling inferior because her next-door neighbor bragged about how much Santa Claus had brought him for Christmas. Since her family was not well-to-do, she did not get many gifts. In her young mind, because Santa was less generous with her, he didn't love her as much as the little boy who lived next door to her. Who would have thought that Santa could be a potential set up for a child's inferiority complex? Therefore, if you as a Christian parent want your little one to look to the Lord as his or her sole source of supply, avoid comparisons, and celebrate the Savior's birthday as it should be celebrated, you must do everything in your power to make sure that Jesus is the holiday focal point.

I woke up the next day with what I had heard the night before weighing heavily on my mind because I have a love for children. I hate to see disappointment in a child's eyes. Who likes to see little kids disappointed? Moreover, who likes to see God disappointed? Unfortunately, when we teach children to believe in Santa, the glory, attention, and focus are taken away from Jesus and transferred to St. Nick. Surely, that has to grieve the heart of God. That's one of the reasons I felt the need to write this book. I want to take whatever action is necessary to shield kids from negative emotions that can easily be avoided and get the focus back on Jesus, our Lord and Savior, on HIS birthday.

I guess my thinking about my own childhood experience is why the Bible study discussion gripped me to such a degree that I continued to think about the topic long after I left the church that Thursday night. I remember how disappointed I was at ten years old when I learned the truth about Santa. Don't get me wrong. I am not angry with my parents, and I don't blame them. They were taught by their parents to believe in Santa, so naturally, they would do the same thing with me and my siblings. I get it. The Santa legacy has been faithfully passed down from one generation to the next. However, I would like to present a new Christmas gift distribution proposal that keeps Christ at the center of the celebration. We must minimize the emphasis on buying, giving, and receiving gifts at the expense of Jesus failing to receive the full attention He truly deserves. Furthermore, I have a sincere desire to spare children everywhere, especially Kingdom Kids, those who are growing up in Christian homes, the disillusionment that is inevitable when they find out who Santa Claus REALLY is. Believing in Santa is destined to set them up for disappointment because, as legendary as he may be, he's not a real person. Jesus, however, IS a real person, and Paul said in Romans 10:11 (NASB), "Whoever believes in Him will not be disappointed."

In light of all of the above, God has given me the strategy that I am going to share with you in this book. My purpose is to give Christian parents an alternative that takes the spotlight off Santa and puts it back on Jesus, "the reason for the season." The focus of the Christmas holiday needs to be shifted from commercialism to Jesus where it rightfully belongs. The ultimate goal is for Christ to get all of the glory He should.

And why shouldn't our Lord be exalted and lifted up? After all, again, it's HIS birthday. If the worthwhile mission of lifting the name and person of Christ is accomplished, John 12:32 will become a reality. Jesus said, "And I, if I am lifted up from the earth, will draw all *peoples* to Myself." That means if Jesus is glorified, then more people will be exposed to the Gospel, which hinges on the event that is at the heart of the Christmas season: the birth of Christ. If unbelievers are exposed to the Gospel, they just might receive Jesus as Lord and Savior, and Satan certainly does not want that to happen, right?

Therefore, I felt compelled to write this book for several reasons: First, I want to present parents with some thought-provoking ideas for keeping the Lord Jesus at the center of the Christmas holiday. Secondly, if the little ones already believe in Santa, my desire is to help parents help their offspring make the transition from focusing on Santa to focusing on Jesus. Thirdly, I feel it's so important to show parents a way to use the Christmas season to fuel the faith of their children and to enhance their future walk with Christ. Finally, my goal is to present a few ideas for celebrating Jesus' birthday in a fun and festive way that keeps Christ at the center of the grand celebration.

I am hoping that when you finish reading what I have written, you will be more excited than ever about celebrating Christmas with your kids. If you will implement the strategies that I have put forth in this book, I believe that the spirit of Christmas will fill your home in an unparalleled way. Additionally, our God will certainly be pleased that you put forth even more effort to keep Christ in Christmas and to give His dear Son the preeminence in your home during Christmas Advent. I pray God will open your heart to the truths that I will share, and I hope you'll be willing to implement the thought-provoking ideas I present in this book during the next Christmas holiday season. I believe, in the end, you'll be glad you did.

What would the original St. Nicholas think of all of the Christmas holiday hoopla that minimizes the birth of JESUS?

CHAPTER 1

WHO WAS ST. NICHOLAS, ANYWAY?

------◆•◆•◆------

Although Santa Claus is a major figure who captures the focus of many during the holiday season, you may be wondering why a book entitled, **Keeping Christ in Christmas** would start with a chapter about Jolly Old St. Nick. You see, I wanted to set the stage regarding why we need to fight to make sure Jesus is at the center of our thoughts and activities during the holiday season. If we are not deliberate and purposeful about giving Jesus absolute preeminence, we are destined to have other things take precedence, and then we fail to experience the manifestation of his presence. Furthermore, we end up missing out on a wonderful opportunity to maximize our joy and heighten our level of intimacy with the Shepherd of our souls.

Therefore, I thought readers might find it quite interesting to know how Santa has evolved over the years into something or someone totally different than his original predecessor, St. Nicholas. I want you to see what the patron saint originally stood for, and how his main focus was giving help to those in need, just as God gave to us when we were in need.

Our heavenly Father gave the gift of Jesus Christ to mankind so that we could be delivered from our sins and avoid eternal damnation. Unfortunately, our focus has ever so slowly been shifted from the real meaning of Christmas, which embodies giving to those who are truly in need, to full-blown Christmas commercialism. Thus, if we're not careful, our focus on Jesus will continue to be transferred from the spiritual to the secular. That's why as believers we must do everything in our power to keep Christ in Christmas and our focus where it belongs.

The Truth about St. Nicholas

According to historical records, St. Nicholas was born 280 A.D. in Patara, a stretch of land that is currently a part of the country of Turkey.[1] Surprisingly enough, he was neither fat nor jolly, but developed a reputation as a "fiery, wiry, and defiant defender of church doctrine during the 'Great Persecution,' when Bibles were put to the torch and priests were made to renounce Christianity or face execution."[2] He became a Christian bishop who helped those who were sick and needy using the inheritance he received from his parents who died when he was a youngster. Because of the miracles that God worked through him and his tireless work for the poverty-stricken and underprivileged, he became well known in other parts of the world. St. Nicholas was believed to have died December 6, 343 AD,[3] and his legacy was allowed to live on in the form of a holiday celebrated on the date of his passing called "feast day."[4] Furthermore, a legend was perpetuated that every year on the day celebrating the anniversary of his death, he would bring gifts to children.

How St. Nicholas Became Associated with Christmas

Although he became a popular saint in Europe, his popularity eventually waned there due to the great turmoil created by the Protestant Reformation that took place in the 1500s. The Dutch, however, refused to give up St. Nicholas as the gift-giver, and he remained a significant figure in Holland. They continued to celebrate the "feast day" of St. Nicholas on December 6 and called him, "Sint Nikolaas." Eventually, he was nicknamed "Sinterklaas." When the tradition was brought to America, his name evolved into "Santa Claus."[5]

While St. Nicholas was alive, Pope Julius I decided the date for the celebration of Jesus' birth would be December 25th, even though there is no way to know the real date for the event. The pontiff probably chose this date because he wanted to Christianize the pagan midwinter festival that usually took place at that time. As time went on, St. Nicholas' "feast day" was shifted and celebrated during the Christmas holiday established by Pope Julius. Thus, the tradition was started where children expected the saint to visit their homes on Christmas Eve, and they would leave fruit, nuts, and sweets out for him to enjoy.[6]

The Evolution of St. Nick in America

Rumor has it that the Dutch people eventually brought their beloved St. Nicholas and his gift-giving practice to America in the 1700s.[7] Researchers have found, however, that there is very little evidence he played any part in their Christmas celebration. It appears St. Nicholas was adopted as an American tradition when Americans became keenly interested in Dutch customs after the Revolutionary War ended.[8]

In 1809 Washington Irving published a book entitled *Knickerbocker's History of New York*. This literary work was the first portrayal of St. Nicholas smoking a pipe and "soaring over rooftops in a flying wagon, delivering presents to good girls and boys and switches to bad ones."[9] But the following year in 1810, Artist Alexander Anderson was commissioned to draw an image of the saint, and he still portrayed him as a religious figure who left gifts in kids' stockings hung by the fireplace.

In 1822 the famous poem entitled, "A Visit from St. Nicholas" or "'Twas the Night Before Christmas" by Clement Clarke Moore was published. At that point, Santa was portrayed as a short, fat, jolly old man who smoked a pipe. He entered the home via the chimney to leave presents for children. The gifts were transported in St. Nick's big sleigh pulled by eight flying reindeer.[10]

In 1881 the great political cartoonist Thomas Nast drew Santa wearing a red suit trimmed in white fur.[11] St. Nick was then said to have his headquarters located at the North Pole where he had a workshop for building toys. Also, the story emerged about his having a book filled with children's names listing who had been naughty or nice.

In the early years, Santa was clothed in other colors other than red, but in the 1940s Santa's red and white suit was cemented by the Coca-Cola Company through their advertisements dressing him in red and white to match the company colors. Norman Rockwell, the famous artist, painted pictures of Santa Claus donned in red and white on many occasions.[12] Thus, the evolution of Santa into the icon that he is today ends here.

The Birth of Commercialism

So there you have it. Santa Claus, who started out as the pious St. Nicholas, has certainly had an extreme makeover down through the years, hasn't he? Also, how the world celebrates the Christmas holiday has evolved as well, hasn't it? I wonder what St. Nicholas would think of all of the Christmas holiday hoopla that minimizes the birth of Jesus and exalts Santa Claus,

Christmas holiday shopping, Christmas decorations, and gluttony. Today's gift-giving does not even reflect what St. Nicholas was about because his mission was to give to people in need. Currently, giving is highly commercialized in that we mainly give purchased gifts to people who really don't need anything.

Unfortunately, at some point in time, a shift took place where the focal point of Christmas became shopping and gift-giving, and Jesus, the greatest gift known to mankind, was stripped of the preeminence He so rightfully deserves. That is how Christmas commercialism was born. Now we make a mad dash to the mall, brave "Black Friday," run up our credit cards, shop online on "Cyber Monday," worry about getting the right gift, get all stressed out with all the other duties and activities that the holiday entails, and forget about the Baby in the manger. We cannot let ourselves get so caught up in this madness that we forget Jesus is truly "*the* reason for the season."

Whose Birthday Is It, Anyway?

Dr. MaryAnn Diorio is an accomplished, multi-award-winning author who writes fiction, non-fiction, and poetry for adults and children. She also happens to be my former life coach. (To find out more about Dr. MaryAnn, please visit www.maryanndiorio.com.) In her blog post "The War on Christmas," she truly captures my sentiments about the societal trend where attention is shifted away from Jesus during the Christmas season. She relays:

> Who would dare denigrate Santa Claus, that kindly old man who brings gifts to children? Yet, Santa Claus has been a deceptive means of drawing people away from the true focus of Jesus Christ, the true and rightful focus of Christmas....The Holy Bible says that Satan [our adversary] presents himself as an "angel of light" (2 Corinthians 11:14). This means that he uses things that look good to entice us.[13]

In other words, the kingdom of darkness is hell-bent on implementing a strategic, well-orchestrated plan of attack on Christmas. The goal is to take the spotlight off Christ in an attempt to get us to focus on everything else but the Savior.

Therefore, Child of God, my purpose in writing this book is to encourage the body of Christ to keep the focus on Jesus where it belongs. Our Lord and Savior Jesus Christ deserves to be fully exalted throughout the Christmas season. After all, it's HIS birthday. I can't stress that enough. He absolutely should not have to put up with competition and share the spotlight on His special day.

Look at it this way: when your birthday comes, don't you want your family and friends to cater to you? You want the celebration to be all about you, right? Of course you do. And Jesus deserves no less than we expect for our own birthdays as we commemorate them annually. Therefore, to further drive my point home, I want to present more food for thought in the next chapter. My goal is to provide one more reason to keep Christ in Christmas and make Him the center of your holiday celebration.

As the Bible says in Luke 14:28, we should count the cost before we start anything we do.

CHAPTER 2

IS IT REALLY WORTH THE RISK?

❖•❖•❖

When children find out the truth about Santa Claus, there can be many different responses depending upon the child. I wanted to get further insight into this, so I decided to do some research on the Internet. I found that most kids take it in stride and go on about their business. They are fine as long as they can get their toy "fix" on Christmas Day. At least that's what I did when I stumbled upon the truth.

My Great Awakening

At ten years old, after writing a letter to Santa and sealing it in an envelope addressed to "The North Pole," I found out on Christmas morning about the reality of St. Nick. Enclosed was my wish list with a ton of things on it that I had my little heart set on for the upcoming day of celebration. I made the huge mistake, however, of telling my parents I wanted only one thing for Christmas.

When I got up on Christmas day in the wee hours of the morning to see what Santa had left me under the tree, to my disappointment, I got the one thing I had shared with my parents that I wanted and some other things I had not asked for. The light bulb came on for me at that moment. I knew my Christmas holidays would never be the same, but I wasn't mad at my parents. I didn't berate them for telling me an untruth. I got over it quickly and simply moved on, as most kids do. But some youngsters may respond differently.

Unintended Outcomes

I have heard about kids who have emotionally concluded if Santa is imaginary, then God must be imaginary. This reaction may seem to be an extreme one, but apparently, it is, indeed, a possibility. Furthermore, I am quite sure this outcome was not anticipated by the parents when they innocently introduced the Santa tradition into their households. Unfortunately, that's how those stories ended.

Dr. MaryAnn Diorio also relays her concern about the possible unintended outcome of harming a child's future relationship with God in her aforementioned blog post, "The War on Christmas," in which she writes:

> Today, parents are criticized if they do not allow their children to go along with the Santa Claus myth. But what happens when children learn that parents did not tell them the truth about Santa Claus? Could this be a reason that, later on, children believe that their parents lied to them about Jesus, too?[1]

Therefore, she and her husband Dom decided to teach their kids that Jesus is the reason for the season. Their success in this endeavor became evident when she was at the mall with her toddler and a woman asked her daughter what she wanted Santa to bring her for Christmas. The little girl looked with confusion at the lady and then turned to her mother and said, "Mommy, doesn't she know the truth about Santa Claus?"[2]

Therefore, parents really need to consider the potential impact that perpetuating the Santa Claus story can have on their children. As the Bible says in Luke 14:28, we should count the cost before we start anything we do. If deliberate and systematic deception could possibly hurt the relationship between parents and children in the future, is the "fun" worth the risk? What if something that seems as simple and harmless as Santa Claus could actually undermine your little one's trust in you as a parental authority? What if children end up concluding Jesus is a farce, or that God isn't real either? Is the temporary "magic" that is experienced on an annual basis really worth it? I think not.

What's the Big Deal?

You might ask, "Why are you making such a big deal out of this?" I am sounding the alarm because I really believe there is a potential risk for children to be spiritually and emotionally impacted. For example, one mom shared a very sad story regarding her child's negative response to learning about the reality of St. Nick. When the youngster found out about the Santa myth, the little one was very adamant about expressing anger, broken-heartedness, and mistrust of the parent. This was evidently a traumatic event for this young person, although every child may not respond this way. However, what if yours does?

Here's one mother's detailed account of an adverse response from a child who received the truth. I interviewed a lady named Lia who graciously shared her personal story of how her daughter found out about Santa. After her child had lost a tooth, Lia told the youngster she should put her tooth underneath her pillow, and the "tooth fairy" would visit her. The little girl then said to her mother with a smirk on her face, "You know some kids say the tooth fairy is their mom." Lia laughed and said, "I guess it was time for you to find out."

After she had let the cat out of the proverbial bag and confirmed her daughter's suspicions, she noticed the child's countenance fell and she looked extremely upset. She then said to her mother, "Wait a minute. What about the Easter Bunny!? What about Santa!? Santa isn't real either!?"

The child then ran into the bathroom, slammed and locked the door, and refused to come out. Feeling betrayed and very humiliated, she yelled at her mother through the door, "Everyone told me it wasn't real, but I believed YOU!" Lia's heart sank. All she wanted to do was create a magical atmosphere in her household during the holiday season.

Then when her son turned ten, she felt it was time for him to find out about Santa, also. She decided to ask her daughter to tell him the truth. His bubble was burst, and he too became very upset when he learned Santa was a figment of his imagination. To this day, both her son and her daughter have vowed never to "deceive" their kids by telling them Santa Claus brings them gifts.

Lia concluded that apparently, she was "too good" at playing Santa. If she had to do it over again, she would have been a "careless Santa," and let the kids find out at a younger age. Perhaps the takeaway is that the longer the myth is perpetuated, the greater the emotional investment children will make. Furthermore, there is an increased potential for them to experience more humiliation and/or betrayal when they do find out the truth. Of course parents mean well, but the choice to introduce Santa into the home can have unintended negative consequences.[3]

Saints, although a child's negative reaction to finding out the truth about Santa may be a one-in-a-million response, is your desire to "create the magic" in this way really worth the risk? If there is any potential whatsoever for your child to be emotionally scarred, or if somehow your relationship with your children could be damaged, is it worth the risk? What if their trust in you as a parent is undermined, and they see you in a negative light, and you are no longer seen as a credible authority figure? Is it worth the risk? Finally, if the truth about Santa Claus could end up causing a child to refuse to believe that God exists and choose atheism, is it worth the risk? I don't think so!

The Choice is Yours

The reason I am writing this chapter is so that you can make an informed choice about what to tell your child. All of these scenarios are potential risks that can be avoided by using the viable alternative that I will present in the following pages of this book. I pray that you will read on with an open mind. Who knows? In the end, how you ultimately choose to celebrate the Christmas holiday could make the difference in your relationship with your child and your child's relationship with God.

Therefore, when you think about the scenarios I have presented in this chapter, the choice you make is a serious matter that can have far-reaching consequences. With that being said, let's move on to the next chapter and take a look at the first thought-provoking idea that will help you keep Jesus at the center of your child's Christmas.

It is more blessed to give than to receive.

Acts 20:35

CHAPTER 3

CULTIVATING A MINDSET OF GIVING VS. GETTING

◆•◆•◆

Christmas is now so commercialized. Before Thanksgiving even gets here, most stores have their Christmas displays in place. Jesus is supposed to be the reason for the season, but our culture here in America continues to push Jesus to the back burner. If we're not careful, we as believers end up running around like chickens with our heads cut off as we "shop until we drop" just like the rest of the world. We get caught up in attending holiday get-togethers where we try to win the "Ugly Christmas Sweater" contest. We need to be mindful, however, lest we clean, cook, and prepare for "The Big Day" and Jesus ends up getting left out.

Many children are so focused on what Santa will bring them. As adults we ask them all the time, "What do you want Santa Claus to bring you for Christmas?" The kids write letters to Santa, sit on his knee at the mall, pour out their heart's desires to St. Nick, and then wait for Christmas morning to come. If they don't get everything they want, they are saddened and disappointed. The truth is that Christmas is not about getting gifts. As my pastor Dr. James Davis would say, "Please don't get upset if you don't get everything you want for Christmas. It's NOT your birthday."

As we have heard numerous times, "Jesus is the reason for the season." Christmas is really about the humongous gift that God gave to the world in the person of Jesus Christ. John 3:16 says, "For God so loved the world that He **gave** [emphasis added] His only begotten Son, that whosoever believeth in him shall not perish but have eternal life." If we want to be like God, we need to be givers. Therefore, children need to be taught to be givers, especially during the holiday season. After all, Jesus Christ did say, "It is more blessed to give than to receive" (Acts 20:35).

Be the Gift

Best-selling author Ann Voskamp has written a book entitled *Be the Gift*. That title is so profound. The question we need to ask ourselves is this: How can I be a gift to the world during the holiday season and beyond? I submit to you that there are three ways we can be a gift to the world: 1) by giving of the financial means that God has given us to bless others; 2) by giving of our God-given time, gifts, and talents to impact the world at large, and 3) by teaching children at an early age to focus on giving versus getting, not only at Christmas but all year long, so they will carry that legacy into adulthood and pass it down to each generation that follows.

Experience Eudaimonic Happiness

But what is the best way to teach children to shift their focus to giving during the holiday season? Give them opportunities to give and see how good it feels. My friend Dr. Christine Bacon has written a book entitled ***The Super Couple: A Formula for Extreme Happiness in Marriage.*** If you would like to improve your marriage, I highly recommend this work. In one of the chapters entitled, "Eudaimonic (pronounced YOU-DUH-MONIC) Happiness," she gives an account of how the opportunity for her, her husband and two little daughters to bless a less fortunate family with Christmas gifts greatly impacted their lives. The type of happiness they experienced by performing an act of kindness for a family in desperate need was described as eudaimonic happiness or the true happiness which is a natural by-product of other-centric thoughts and practices. She states that the rewards of this type of happiness are intrinsic, long-term and actually increase as we continue the noble practice of putting others before ourselves.[1]

To illustrate the concept of teaching children to shift their focus from getting gifts to giving and being a gift, I'd like to present to you the heartwarming and thought-provoking excerpt from the aforementioned chapter in her book that I believe will successfully drive the point home. She writes:

My family used to attend a church that collected food and gifts for the poorest of the poor in our city and delivered those gifts to each family a few days prior to the Christmas holiday....On one particular Christmas week my family was given grocery bags filled with a turkey or ham, enough groceries for a complete, yet humble, Christmas dinner for a family of seven and fourteen individually wrapped gifts—two per person—each marked with the tags from the Angel Tree [Ministry]. We were sent to the poorest (and dare I say the most dangerous) part of our city with nothing more than the address of the recipients. My husband, myself, and both of our daughters were together on this brisk, dark winter day and I must admit, we were in a hurry to do what it was we needed to do and quickly leave for whatever event we had next on our schedule for that day, you know, something extremely important like dinner with friends or maybe a date with our television and a Green Bay Packers game...or more Christmas shopping. Imperative stuff. I could see my daughters' bored expressions through the rearview mirror as we headed to our destination— looks that said, "Hurry up and get this over with. Why did you have to take us anyway? You could have done this without us." My daughters were seven and ten at the time.

As we pulled up to the ill-repaired building on a city block where every other home was equally as worn and dilapidated, I got out of the car and slowly walked up the broken steps to the front entrance. I knocked on the door and it was partially and apprehensively opened by a sweet and well-mannered twelve-year-old boy who managed a gentle "Hi." When I asked if his mom was home he said she was in the restroom—obviously a [routine] response from a child who'd likely been left alone frequently while his mother was probably at work earning whatever she could to feed her family. Based on the ages and genders on the Angel tags, we knew there was no adult male in this household.

After introducing myself I let him know that [we] were there to bring them a few [gifts] for Christmas and asked if it would be okay for us to bring them up to the front door and place them on the porch?

"I guess so."

With that he opened the door widely, exposing a house with only a few pieces of furniture: a couch, an end table and a lampstand. There were no rugs, only sheets for curtains, only handmade children's artwork on the walls, a small television propped on the seat of a wooden chair and, most notably, a very small "Charlie Brown" Christmas tree in the corner of the room with no tree skirt and no presents underneath—not even one. On it was a strand or two of lights and a smattering of handmade, paper ornaments. My heart was immediately saddened to know that people had to live with so little while my children had never gone a day without a meal or material pleasures. I quickly glanced down the hallway and noticed that the scarcity of "stuff" extended far beyond what I saw in front of me.

At my signal, my husband then exited the car with the two bags of groceries in each arm and handed them to the young boy— his face revealing a look of bewilderment at the unexpected gift. "These are for your

Christmas dinner" he quietly told the boy and turned to retrieve the gifts from the trunk. The young boy and I followed him. My daughters now exited the car, seemingly gaining a greater awareness of our mission and turned to meet us at the now open trunk. My husband placed a gift in Gabrielle's hands—my seven-year-old—a couple more gifts into the arms of my ten-year-old Jessica, and two more into the arms of this young boy. With gifts in my husband's and my arms as well, we followed him up to his front door where he took the time to place each gift gently under the tree, his look of astonishment growing ever more evident. As we handed them to him we read the tags, "This one is for a three-year-old girl."*

"Oh, that's my baby sister Bella!"

"And this one says a seven-year-old boy."

"That's Sam's! That must be Sam's! Wow, that looks pretty big!"

We continued this gift-handling and identification process until we got to the very last presents. And I promise you not for the sake of exaggerating a story for this book but rather, as if divinely planned the very last two gifts tied together with ribbon said "twelve-year-old boy." As this final gift was handed to this sweet and gentle boy, he looked up and said, "For me? There's one for me too?" It seemed as if in his tender heart that though he saw gifts for each of his family members, including his mother, something deep down prevented him from assuming there'd be one for him as well. Possibly a lifetime of barren Christmases where few, if any, gifts were ever found under the tree Christmas morning, he had conditioned himself to expect nothing. I will never forget how he clutched this shirt-box sized gift to his chest and just stood there for what seemed like five minutes (but was probably more like five seconds). Immediately thereafter the largest smile ever seen on a twelve-year-old stretched across his beautiful face—the kind of happy smile that stays on your face the entire day of your wedding or after you've just delivered your newborn baby.

We wished him a merry Christmas and from our respective seats in our car, we watched him until he entered his house [and reminded] him not to forget to lock the door behind him. As my husband pulled away, our car remained blessedly silent, for none of us wanted to speak and lose the spirit of what we had just experienced—each of us obviously touched by the emotionally powerful interchange we had just been a part of. Finally, after about five minutes, I heard the voice of my seven-year-old, "Can we do that again next year?" I knew exactly what she meant, and yes, we absolutely would do that again next year.

What my daughter articulated and we all felt that day was the intrinsic by-product of eudemonic happiness—the highest human good—whereupon we put someone else's needs before our own and our souls began to flourish. We were happy—truly happy. Here it is more than two decades later and that short fifteen-minute interchange is still seared in my mind's eye as if it had just occurred last Christmas.[2]

This story reveals there was a shift in the Bacon children's thinking. They saw that what Jesus said in Acts 20:35 is true: It IS more blessed to give than to receive. They got it. Likewise, we have to impress upon children the importance of recognizing that while getting the gifts they desire on Christmas morning is exciting, they must be mindful that there are people who are not as fortunate as they are. Also, we need to help them see that at the moment they give, they are being most like God. John 3:16 says, "For God so loved the world, that He **gave** [emphasis added] His only begotten Son." Jesus said in Matthew 20:28 (NASB), "The Son of Man did not come to be served, but to serve, and to **give** [emphasis added] his life as a ransom for many." Therefore, through the blessed opportunities you afford them to be givers to those in need at holiday time, they become a gift to others and get the opportunity to experience the joy of spreading joy.

Give to Those in Need

Parents, if you really want to keep Christ in Christmas, help your children to focus on giving for the purpose of positively impacting the lives of others. That means not just giving to people who have everything and don't need anything. Find ways to give of your time, talents and treasure as a family unit. Seek out those in need, those who are less fortunate. Give to those who have very little hope at Christmastime. Give to those who are poverty-stricken and those who can't afford to buy toys for their kids. It is in this type of giving you will find your greatest sense of fulfillment. Furthermore, you will help your kids to be more appreciative of what they do receive for

Christmas and also help them to change their whole perspective on giving all year long.

Perhaps your child may decide to give away gently used toys they no longer play with. Or maybe they want to use some of their own money to buy a small gift for another child, even if it's from the dollar store. Maybe they want to volunteer their time to help the needy in some way. Present alternatives, and help them decide. The goal is to encourage them to shift their main focus from getting to giving because when they do, they model Jesus. He made the ultimate sacrifice and gave His life, the most wonderful gift ever given.

Therefore, I challenge you to think of more ways that you and your family can give generously to those in need during the holiday season. Teaching children to focus on meeting the needs of others is a novel mindset that certainly differs from the general world view. So as a family, if you want to keep Christ in Christmas, seek out the less fortunate and give gifts to them. Volunteer your time to causes that will help others. Be sensitive to the Holy Spirit and use your gifts and talents to bless those He leads you to bless. With that being said, now it's time to look at another thought-provoking idea in the next chapter that is sure to help you keep the focus on our Lord and Savior during one of the most sacred times of the year.

*James 1:17 says,
"Every good gift and every perfect gift is from above, and comes down from the Father of lights."*

CHAPTER 4

MAKING JESUS THE GIFT-GIVER

Kids love Christmas. I'm sure many children would say Christmastime is their most favorite time of the year. Why? Because it's so magical! They enjoy the festivities, especially receiving gifts. Most kids look forward to going to the mall and sitting on Santa's knee and telling him what they want for Christmas. The problem is that Jesus is the reason for the season, but Santa ends up being at the center of children's thoughts during the holidays instead of Jesus. Unfortunately, most children end up focusing on getting gifts, and not the Giver of all gifts.

Let's flashback to the Bible study conversation at the beginning of this book that started all of this. After I left church on that Thursday night following the discussion about whether or not to teach kids that Santa brings their gifts after they go to bed on Christmas Eve, I was genuinely disturbed. I fell asleep with the thoughts about how to rectify this situation weighing heavily on my mind. When I woke up the next morning, God began to bring to my remembrance ideas about how to keep Christ in Christmas He had laid upon my heart many years ago.

Here is a novel idea I would like to propose: Make **Jesus the Gift-giver** for the holidays instead of Santa. What if you told your kids that Jesus is the One Who will bring their gifts this year? I dare you to try this as an experiment. You see, kids love gifts. They don't care where they come from as long as they see gifts under the tree. If you tell them that Jesus brought the gifts, their focus stays on Him and the gifts, not on Santa and the gifts. Psalm 16:8 says, "I have set the Lord always before me;

Because *He is* at my right hand I shall not be moved." When you encourage them at a young age to keep their focus on Jesus as much as possible, you are laying a good spiritual foundation upon which they can build their faith later in life.

When you think about it, Jesus DOES bring the gifts. After all, James 1:17 says, "Every good gift and every perfect gift is from above, and comes down from the Father of lights." Therefore, even when the kids believe Santa brought their gifts, who REALLY brought those gifts? Ultimately, GOD, the Father. He is also Jehovah Jireh, our Provider. So, since the Father and the Son are one and the same, if you told your children that Jesus instead of Santa will bring the gifts while they sleep, you would certainly be telling the truth, right? Look at it this way, if you are a Christian, Jesus lives in you. So as you put the gifts under the tree, Jesus REALLY is the ultimate Gift-giver THROUGH YOU.

I know that making Jesus the Gift-giver is a novel concept. You may be resistant to the idea because Santa has been a tradition that has been passed down in your family for generations. However, I pray you will not shut down on me and close the book yet. Please hear me out! There are several advantages to this approach of having Jesus be the Gift-giver.

The Element of Wonder and Surprise Still Remains

There is still the element of wonder and surprise, but not at the expense of removing Jesus from the center of the holiday. When the children are tucked into bed on Christmas Eve, they will still probably have a hard time falling asleep and will be looking forward to getting the gifts that Jesus Himself will bring. When they get up on Christmas morning, they will have the same excitement that comes with getting gifts from Santa. Wouldn't it be better to have your kids shower their attention and gratefulness onto Jesus?

Truthfulness and Sincerity Are Maintained

When you tell your kids Jesus brought their gifts, you remain truthful. Although you buy the gifts and put them under the tree, and as I mentioned previously, if you are a Christian, Jesus does actually live in you, and He is using YOU to put the gifts under the Christmas tree! Galatians 2:20 (NASB) says, "I have been crucified with Christ; and it is no longer I who live, but Christ lives in me; and the *life* which I now live in the flesh I live by faith in the Son of God, who loved me and gave Himself up for me." Therefore, again, the Lord Jesus is ultimately the Gift-giver THROUGH YOU.

So giving Jesus the credit for the gifts allows parents to keep a clear conscience. Let's face it. It's important to set a good example and tell kids the truth because Ephesians 4:25 says,

"Therefore, putting away lying, '*Let* each one *of you* speak truth with his neighbor.'" If a parent tells a child it's not OK to lie, and then turns around and tells that child Santa Claus brought the gifts, how does the Holy Spirit feel about that? Therefore, when Jesus is the Gift-giver, sincerity and honesty are maintained.

The Focus Remains on Jesus as the Reason for the Season

When Jesus is the Gift-giver, this allows the focus to remain on the Savior as the real reason for the holiday season. As I mentioned previously, this is so important because Jesus said in John 12:32, "And I, if I am lifted up from the earth, will draw all *peoples* to Myself." In other words, if Jesus is the focal point, people will be drawn to Him. Therefore, when you make Christ your family's main focus during the Christmas holiday, you create a wonderful opportunity for those in your sphere of influence to be drawn to Him.

Additionally, when we allow our children to focus on Santa Claus instead of on Jesus, we dilute the power of our ability to witness to the world because we have embraced the world's commercialistic view. When we exalt Santa, we allow the world to set the pace for our families. We should be the leaders not the followers because Deuteronomy 28:13 says we are "the head and not the tail." The head leads, the tail follows. Amen? Furthermore, I John 2:15 says, "Do not love the world or the things in the world." That's why we need to make up our minds that we will exalt Jesus, and only Jesus, if we want the anointing for evangelism to operate in our lives during the holiday and every day.

Dependence on God Is Encouraged

As you point children to Jesus as the Gift-giver, you plant a seed which will ultimately encourage them to depend on God and not upon man for provision. For example, take a look at Genesis 22:13-14 (NIV), which relays how God provided a sacrifice so that Abraham would not have to sacrifice his son Isaac:

> Abraham looked up and there in a thicket he saw a ram caught by its horns. He went over and took the ram and sacrificed it as a burnt offering instead of his son. So Abraham called that place The Lord Will Provide. And to this day it is said, "On the mountain of the Lord it will be provided."

Conversely, when you think about it, if we encourage kids to look to Santa for what they want and need versus God, that's really a form of idolatry. Yes, idolatry. St. Nick may be make-believe to us, but the little ones actually believe what we tell them. In their little minds, Santa is for real. We have to keep in mind that Exodus 20:3 says, "You shall have no other gods before Me." That is all the more reason to keep Christ in Christmas.

God Is Viewed as the Source of Supply

When you encourage your child to look to Jesus for his or her gifts, you align yourself with what is written in Philippians 4:19: "And my God shall supply all your need according to His riches in glory by Christ Jesus." Also, Psalms 37:4 says, "Delight yourself also in the LORD, And HE [emphasis added] shall give you the desires of your heart." Therefore, teaching children to ask Jesus for their gifts gives them the awesome opportunity to see God give them the desires of their hearts. This will reinforce their trust and faith in Him at an early age. Furthermore, they will be able to see the truth in Matthew 21:22 which states, "And whatever things you ask in prayer, believing, you will receive." Consequently, when prayers are answered, their faith will be strengthened.

The Discipline of Prayer Is Reinforced

When you encourage your child to pray and ask Jesus for gifts, you actively reinforce the discipline of prayer. I Thessalonians 5:17 tells us to "pray without ceasing." Therefore, prayer should be like breathing, and praying to Jesus instead of writing to Santa will be much more fruitful if you want to enhance your child's spirituality. By making Jesus the center of the holiday season, parents create an opportunity for children to practice praying, exercise their faith, and experience the joy that comes with seeing their prayers answered. Another added bonus is that kids will cultivate their relationship with God through prayer.

Furthermore, Jesus did say in Matthew 18:19 (NASB), "Again I say to you, that if two of you agree on earth about anything that they may ask, it shall be done for them by My Father who is in heaven." When you kneel down with your child in a special prayer session, specifically for the purpose of asking Jesus for Christmas gifts, and agree with that child about what he or she wants to receive, you provide a prayer model for your child and give him the opportunity to see that God's Word does work. The youngster will see firsthand the truth of Matthew 7:11 (NIV) which says, "How much more will your Father in heaven give good gifts to those who ask him!"

God Gets the Glory

When your children ask Jesus to give them gifts through prayer and their prayers are answered, our God is glorified. John 14:13 says, "And whatsoever you ask in My name, that I will do, that the Father may be glorified in the Son." Furthermore, Isaiah 42:8 says, "I *am* the LORD, that *is* My name; And My glory I will not give to another, Nor My praise to carved images." But by teaching kids to ask Santa for what they want, we are stripping God of the opportunity to get the glory that He rightly deserves. When God is robbed, surely that is not a good thing. The Father deserves better. Don't you agree?

Kids Have a Witnessing Tool

A final benefit of having Jesus replace Santa as the Gift-giver is that this provides a tool for children to use to witness to their little friends. Mark 16:15 (NASB) says, "Go into all the world and preach the gospel to all creation." When your child's friends mention the gifts that Santa brought, your son or daughter will be able to tell them, "Santa doesn't bring us gifts, Jesus brings our gifts," and that will open up a door to talk about Jesus. Perhaps some of their friends will ask Who Jesus is and create an opportunity for a discussion about the Lord.

So as you can see, there are many advantages to making Jesus the Gift-giver during the holiday season. When you think about it, believing in Santa counteracts the truths that will build your child's faith on several levels. However, believing in Jesus as the holiday Gift-giver will fuel their faith and provide a foundation for their relationship with Him. Finally, through this model, children will be more likely to not only look to Jesus to provide their gifts at Christmastime, but look to Him to provide their needs and wants all year round.

I know that this novel idea I've presented is a radical concept for those who have been used to having St. Nick be the one to bring gifts. The Santa tradition has gone on for generations, and I know that change is hard sometimes. The ideas in this book may not be received by everyone. However, this radical concept is for radical Christians who are determined to escape Christmas commercialism, want to pay homage to the Savior that He so rightfully deserves, and want to raise their children in the nurture and admonition of the Lord.

Are you up for the challenge? Are you ready to try something new this Christmas? I pray that you are, and in the next chapter, if you already have children who believe in Santa, I will show you how to facilitate the transition of your child's focus upon St. Nick to a focus upon the King of kings.

*Kids love gifts,
and they don't care
how they get them.*

CHAPTER 5

MAKING THE TRANSITION FROM SANTA TO JESUS

If you are currently childless but planning to have children, what will you do about Santa Claus when celebrating Christmas with your future little sweetie pies? Honestly, you are at a really good place because implementing the alternative I proposed in Chapter 4 will be easier when your children have never been introduced to Santa. Your kids will joyfully know Jesus as the Gift-giver right from the very beginning.

However, what if you have already introduced your kids to Santa, they have written letters, sat on his lap at the mall, and awakened only to see that he had blessed them with their heart's desire? It is never too late for you to introduce Jesus as the Gift-giver and keep Him at the center of your celebration. It will just take a little effort to indoctrinate the children to the new holiday focal point, Jesus Himself.

You see, making the transition from Santa to Jesus is not rocket science. As I stated previously, kids love gifts, and they don't care how they get them. If you set the pace and lead them, they will fall right in line with what you present to them. Therefore, your goal is to simply transfer the focus and attention from Santa to Jesus. Below, I've laid out the step-by-step process you can use to assist your child in shifting his or her focus to Jesus as the main Gift-giver for the holiday season.

The Transition Process

1. This year you won't ask your child, "What do you want Santa Claus to bring you for Christmas?" As December 25th approaches, you can kick off the transition process as the little one begins to talk about toys he or

she would like to receive. You can start the ball rolling by saying, "We are going to pray and ask *Jesus* to bring our gifts this year. So what do you want *Jesus* to bring you for Christmas?" You can add, "Isn't it wonderful that *Jesus* wants to give you gifts, and it's HIS birthday?"

2. If your child already believes in Santa, do NOT say that Santa doesn't exist, just tell him the following: "[Child's Name], instead of asking Santa for gifts this year, we are going to ask *Jesus* for the gifts we want. *Jesus* is the one Who gives us what we need and want when we ask. So we are going to pray, ask *Jesus* for what we want for Christmas, and thank Him for the gifts He's going to bring, OK?"

One reason you don't want to say Santa does not exist is that you do not want your child to tell other children and cause their parents to have to explain. Parents should be in control of when and how their kids receive information about Santa. This will help you avoid a confrontation about this issue with other parents.

3. Charge each family member to decide on a special offering or birthday gift to be given to Jesus that is either tangible and/or intangible during the holiday season.

   Some examples of tangible gifts:
   - Give a special offering or monetary gift to a person or charity.
   - Allow your children to give away some of their old toys to kids at a shelter.
   - Visit a nursing home and take gifts for the residents (e.g., toiletries, snacks, the children's personal artwork, or homemade Christmas cards).
   - Find a needy family and give them a box or bags containing the groceries needed to prepare a holiday meal.

   Some examples of intangible gifts:
   - The family can volunteer to serve at a soup kitchen or shelter.

- The child may agree to help dad or mom with a chore.
- The child will do his chores without being asked in obedience to their parents and an effort to be pleasing to Jesus.
- The child can agree to be extra nice to a sibling or friend.

4. To set the stage for why the family will focus on Jesus as the Giver of gifts this year, share a few of the following scriptures with your child on different occasions leading up to December 25th:

- **Matthew 2:7-11 (NIV)**
  Then Herod called the Magi secretly and found out from them the exact time the star had appeared. He sent them to Bethlehem and said, "Go and search carefully for the child. As soon as you find him, report to me, so that I too may go and worship him."

  After they had heard the king, they went on their way, and the star they had seen when it rose went ahead of them until it stopped over the place where the child was. When they saw the star, they were overjoyed. On coming to the house, they saw the child with his mother Mary, and they bowed down and worshiped him. Then they opened their treasures and presented him with gifts of gold, frankincense and myrrh.

The age-old custom of giving and receiving Christmas presents was established to remind us of the presents of frankincense, gold, and myrrh the Wise Men gave to Jesus. The meaning of each of these precious gifts is as follows:

- Frankincense was a perfume used in Jewish worship and, as a gift, it showed that people would worship Jesus [as Lord].

- Gold was associated with kings, and Christians believe that Jesus is the King of kings.
- Myrrh was a perfume that was put on dead bodies to make them smell nice and, as a gift, it showed that Jesus would suffer and die.[1]

- **John 3:16 (NIV)**
  "For God so loved the world that he gave his one and only Son, that whoever believes in him shall not perish but have eternal life." (Tell the little ones, "Since God gave His Son as a gift to the world, we should learn to be givers also. Baby Jesus was a gift from God, but now Jesus is all grown up and wants to give us gifts! Isn't that great?")

- **James 1:17**
  "Every good gift and every perfect gift is from above." (Tell your child, "This means that every gift we get comes from Heaven. Every good gift we receive comes from God.

That's why we are going to ask Jesus to bring our gifts.")

- **Philippians 4:19**
  "And my God shall supply all your need according to His riches in glory by Christ Jesus." (When we ask Jesus for gifts, we are aligned with God's Word. When children are directed to request toys from Santa, we incorrectly teach that Santa is the source of supply. Therefore, I encourage you to tell your child, "God supplies our needs and wants, NOT Santa.")

- **James 4:2**
  "You do not have because you do not ask." (We must teach children if they want something they can ask Jesus for it.)

- **John 20:19 (NIV)**
  "On the evening of that first day of the week, when the disciples were together, with the doors locked for fear of the Jewish leaders, Jesus came and stood among them

and said, 'Peace be with you!'" (This scripture can be used to show that Jesus doesn't need a chimney to get into the house. He can even come through locked doors.)

- **II Corinthians 10:12 (NIV)**
"We do not dare to classify or compare ourselves with some who commend themselves. When they measure themselves by themselves and compare themselves with themselves, they are not wise." (Paul surely gave us food for thought with this quote. When kids embrace this principle, they will be less apt to feel "shortchanged" if their friends get a lot of gifts from "Santa" and they don't because of a difficult financial situation. We have to teach them early on to avoid the comparison trap. Because Jesus uniquely loves each of us, He gives us what we need and the wants we can handle. Also, we need to help children shift their focus to being a blessing to others and not only looking to receive.)

The above foundational scriptures will be very instrumental in helping your child look to Jesus as the Gift-giver and keep Christ in Christmas. Once you have read and explained them to your child in a way he or she can understand, you will be well on your way to making the transition where Christ is the center of your Christmas celebration. Your first task is to help your child adopt a new mindset based upon the Word of God instead of the world's commercialism. Then you can begin to practice some new traditions and enjoy your Christmas holiday with a new-found fervor that comes with your new focal point: Jesus.

The next chapter presents a few more thought-provoking ideas to help keep Christ at the center of your family's Christmas holiday. These activities will help to unify your family, give you events around which to fellowship, and also help each of you as individuals to draw closer to the Savior during Advent. I pray that as you implement the suggestions, you will start some family traditions that will be passed down from generation to generation.

The more you exalt Jesus, the more His presence will permeate your home.

CHAPTER 6

KEEPING CHRIST AT THE CENTER

Once you have made the shift to having your kids focus on Christ during the Christmas season by praying to Jesus and believing that He will provide their gifts, I would like to encourage you to start some new Christmas traditions in your home that I will present in the following pages. The suggested activities will promote the maintenance of a festive atmosphere and will also exalt Jesus in the process. If you will implement these ideas, you'll invite the presence of God to manifest to a greater degree in your home, and the peace of God will be more evident because Jesus will definitely feel warmly welcomed.

Activities for the Days Leading up to Christmas Eve

In her online article "Ways to Keep Christ in Christmas," Marketing Director of the website Thedatingdivas.com, Becca, gives some great ideas for keeping Jesus at the center of your family's Christmas holiday:

o **Play Christ-centered Christmas music throughout the household.** There's nothing like Christmas carols with Jesus as the central theme to help you and your family get in the holiday spirit. Music can be a great way to anchor our thoughts on the Savior in the days leading up to Advent.

o **Read Christ-centered Christmas holiday books about Jesus' birth with your kids.** Some good choices are as follows:

- *'Twas the Night Before Jesus* – The familiar rhyme is brought to life with the beautiful Christmas story.

- ***J Is for Jesus: The Sweetest Story Ever Told*** – A sweet story to remind little ones that the candy cane represents Jesus' birth and His gospel message too.
- ***Room for a Little One: A Christmas Tale*** – Kind Ox invites one visitor after another into the shelter of his stable on a cold winter night.[1]

Here are some other ideas you may want to consider implementing during the time leading up to Christmas Eve:

- **Put up birthday decorations**. In addition to the Christmas tree and other traditional holiday decorations, decorate as if you are having a birthday party. Hang balloons and streamers in red, white and green. Put up a "Happy Birthday, Jesus!" banner. The more festive the atmosphere, the better.

- **Consider instituting a "three-gift rule."** I happened to stumble on a blog post by

Lauren Greutman at LaurenGreutman.com entitled, "Why My Kids Get Only 3 Gifts at Christmas." She is a consumer savings expert who recognizes the financial struggle parents face in staying on budget during the holidays. Lauren instituted the three-gift rule in her home for her four children for Christmas, and the rationale she uses to explain the rule to her kids is that Jesus got three gifts: gold, frankincense and myrrh. This approach helps them to focus on Jesus, to think carefully, and to be selective about what they want for Christmas. It also keeps parents from being so stressed out over excessive holiday spending. Lauren also cites guidelines for the children's choices for the gifts: something they want, something they need, something to wear, or something to read. I love this poetic format that makes the guidelines very easy to remember. Additionally, the three-gift rule helps to put a tremendous damper on the commercialism that usually is the focus of the Christmas holiday.[2]

- **Pray together as a family.** Have a family meeting where the children are led in prayer and thanksgiving for the gifts they want Jesus to bring. At this point the children may have previously told you what they want for Christmas. However, this is your opportunity to pray in agreement with one another. The children should ask Jesus for the things they want and believe they have received as noted in Mark 11:24 (NIV) which states: "Therefore I tell you, whatever you ask for in prayer, believe that you have received it, and it will be yours." This family session can be held a few weeks before Christmas, and you may even want to repeat the prayer on Christmas Eve.

- **Reveal gifts to be given to Jesus.** Ask each person to reveal the special offering or gift (tangible and/or intangible) that he or she will give as a birthday present to Jesus as mentioned in Chapter 5. This will help kids to stay balanced and focused on the noble virtue of giving during the holiday season.

This activity should probably be done two to three weeks before Christmas Eve so that you will have time to plan for volunteer outings and other creative ways each family member has decided to give to those in your household and others in need.

Activities for Christmas Eve

The following Christ-centered family activities, designed to help you to stay focused on Jesus in preparation for His birthday, can be done on Christmas Eve:

- **On Christmas Eve, read and discuss the Christmas Story in Luke 2:1-20 together as a family.** This activity will serve as a great reminder of the real reason for the celebration. At any given point you can stop and expound on or ask the kids questions about what you have read to make sure they understand the biblical storyline and its significance. Let this passage be used to guide you into your special Christmas Eve devotional time with your family.

Luke 2:1-20

1 And it came to pass in those days that a decree went out from Caesar Augustus that all the world should be registered.

2 This census first took place while Quirinius was governing Syria.

3 So all went to be registered, everyone to his own city.

4 Joseph also went up from Galilee, out of the city of Nazareth, into Judea, to the city of David, which is called Bethlehem, because he was of the house and lineage of David,

5 to be registered with Mary, his betrothed wife, who was with child.

6 So it was, that while they were there, the days were completed for her to be delivered.

7 And she brought forth her firstborn Son, and wrapped Him in swaddling cloths, and laid Him in a manger, because there was no room for them in the inn.

8 Now there were in the same country shepherds living out in the fields, keeping watch over their flock by night.

9 And behold, an angel of the Lord stood before them, and the glory of the Lord shone around them, and they were greatly afraid.

10 Then the angel said to them, "Do not be afraid, for behold, I bring you good tidings of great joy which will be to all people.

11 For there is born to you this day in the city of David a Savior, who is Christ the Lord.

12 And this will be the sign to you: You will find a Babe wrapped in swaddling cloths, lying in a manger."

13 And suddenly there was with the angel a multitude of the heavenly host praising God and saying:

14 "Glory to God in the highest, And on earth peace, goodwill toward men!"

15 So it was, when the angels had gone away from them into heaven, that the shepherds said to one another, "Let us now go to Bethlehem and see this thing that has come to pass, which the Lord has made known to us."

16 And they came with haste and found Mary and Joseph, and the Babe lying in a manger.

17 Now when they had seen Him, they made widely known the saying which was told them concerning this Child.

18 And all those who heard it marveled at those things which were told them by the shepherds.

19 But Mary kept all these things and pondered them in her heart.

20 Then the shepherds returned, glorifying and praising God for all the things that they had heard and seen, as it was told them.

o **Rent Christ-centered Christmas videos and watch them together as a family.** Some excellent possibilities might include **The Star**, **A Charlie Brown Christmas**, or **Veggie Tales: The Ultimate Christmas Collection,** all of which have strong faith-based messages. Watching and discussing great Christmas holiday movie classics is an awesome way to spend time with your family on a Christmas Eve.

o **Bake a birthday cake as a family for Jesus.** As you work on this project together (mixing, baking and frosting the cake), family fellowship and unity are fostered. Be sure to put candles on the cake so that on Christmas Day they can be lit as you sing the Happy Birthday Song to Jesus. Once you have eaten Christmas dinner, you can pull out the cake and have dessert! Yum![3]

Activities for Christmas Day

On Christmas Day, the family can participate in the following activities that can be done to create some great family traditions and maintain momentum as you purposefully attempt to keep Christ in Christmas:

- **Open your gifts together.** When you wake up on Christmas morning, together as a family, open the gifts that Jesus brought. Make it a point to have each family member say "Thank You, Jesus!" for each one. This will foster the attitude of gratitude that our Lord greatly appreciates as exemplified in Luke 17:11-19 when the one leper came back to thank Jesus for healing him.

- **Give Jesus a place at the dinner table.** At Christmas mealtime, have an empty place setting available for Jesus. This just serves as a tangible reminder that Jesus is present, even though you can't see Him. You may even want to give Him a special place at the head of the table. This is symbolic that He is the head of the home.

o **Have a birthday party for Jesus!** Make sure birthday party favors are available for the celebration (e.g. noise makers, hats, etc.). After all, it's Jesus' birthday! Since kids love parties, you want to make sure they have a lot of fun. This will make the holiday more memorable for them.[4]

o **Bring out the cake!** After Christmas dinner light the candles on Jesus' birthday cake and sing the Happy Birthday Song to Him. Let everyone blow out the candles together, and then you can serve the birthday cake for dessert.

o **Let the games begin!** After dinner (or at some time during the day), play games with the children as a family. Allow them to have your full attention. This holiday game session will be well worth the investment of your time because you are attempting to build a relationship with your children and foster a deep connection through fun and fellowship. Furthermore, when you play games and have fun with your kids, they will remember that for years to come.

I strongly believe if you will implement these suggestions during the Christmas holiday, the payoff will be huge. Maybe you have traditions that you are already practicing that give Jesus first place. I hope that you will add these to your repertoire because, as you well know, the more you exalt Jesus, the more His presence will permeate your home. Your little ones will follow your lead and, hopefully, they will be encouraged to give Jesus first place in their lives. Who knows? They may even keep the tradition going within their homes when they have kids of their own. If so, that's one way you will truly know that the effort you put forth to keep Christ in Christmas was not in vain. You'll have left a wonderful legacy!

CHAPTER 7

'TWAS THE NIGHT BEFORE JESUS' BIRTHDAY

◆·◆·◆

I love poetry. In fact I am a poet. They call me "The Purposeful Poet" because my purpose is to encourage, uplift and inspire people to be their best for Christ. As a child, I loved the poem, ***A Visit from St. Nick*** by Clement Clarke Moore. You know, the one that starts, "'Twas the night before Christmas, and all through the house, Not a creature was stirring not even a mouse." That poem is so cleverly written! Now, however, since I am proposing that Christ be the Gift-giver at Christmas instead of Santa, I felt it would only be appropriate to revamp the poem I appreciated so much as a child and make Christ the center of it.

Therefore, I decided to write a poem called, **"'Twas the Night Before Jesus' Birthday."** In this poem I wanted to exalt Jesus and highlight His generosity and provision of Christmas gifts for a family who gave Him first place in their lives during the holiday season. I pray that you will enjoy my Christ-centered version of Mr. Moore's classic poem. I pray you will consider starting the tradition of reading this holiday poem to your children on Christmas Eve.

'TWAS THE NIGHT BEFORE JESUS' BIRTHDAY

'Twas the night before Jesus' birthday,
  and all through the house
Was the laughter and joy of my kids and my
  spouse.
Our house, decorated with love and great care,
Was prepared for His presence to manifest
  there.
The children then fell asleep; they were
  tucked into bed,
Dreams of Xboxes and Barbies danced in their
  heads,

My wife in her nightgown, and I in my pajamas,
Anticipated tomorrow's excitement and drama.
We laid down to rest for the big celebration
That would be filled with happiness and jubilation,
Because our Savior was born and laid in a manger
To make sure that our souls were rescued from danger.
As we slept, Jesus showed up in bodily form,
Glanced around the room to see our house adorned
With all of the decorations we'd put up for Him
To celebrate His birthday with vigor and vim.
As I woke from my sleep, Jesus gently called me
To come fellowship with Him and to bow my knee,
To worship Him, and spend quality time,
To be in His presence was so sublime.
I then sat down to talk with Him for a few,
Like two friends, we conversed, as we often do.

He showed me in His Word some things anew,
He told me to seek His face, and His will pursue.
Then He pointed to gifts under the Christmas tree
He had lovingly picked out for our family.
And suddenly, great joy sprang up in my heart,
I praised Him for the gifts He did impart,
He had blessed us mightily with presents galore,
For the kids and my wife, there was such glee in store.
He left me speechless because He'd been so good,
He had richly blessed us as a good Father would,
I then exclaimed as I worshiped and praised,
I fell on my knees with both my hands raised,
I said, "Thank You, Lord, for the gifts You have brought;
Thank You for the valuable lesson You've taught!
You're the reason for the season, and You are the center;

It's all about You, as into Advent we enter.
I trust You for provision, and not Santa Claus,
That is why I celebrate Christmas and take
 time to pause
To reflect on why You came from Heaven to
 Earth,
So that I can tell others about the Virgin Birth.
Born to die for our sins on a rugged cross,
You came to seek and save that which was
 lost,
I am so grateful for what You've done for me,
You died so that I could be radically set free."
His presence remained, and our home filled
 with peace,
I could hardly wait for the long night to cease.
When the kids would see the gifts Jesus left for
 them,
He would get all the glory, and only Him.
His generosity floored me; this was HIS
 birthday!
Yet He saw fit to bless us when we did pray.
But the greatest gift that He gave was His
 blood that He shed,

I can never repay Him for how He suffered and bled.
I told Him, "Thank You! Happy Birthday!" before I went to bed,
I'd never forget the things Jesus had said,
He's to be exalted far above Santa Claus,
And I need to remember that He is The Boss.
Then Jesus looked at me as He exclaimed with delight,
"Merry Christmas to you, and I bid you good night!"

CONCLUSION

In **Keeping Christ in Christmas**, I've done my best to give you a multi-faceted strategy for keeping Jesus at the Center of your children's Christmas holiday season. Making the transition from Santa to Jesus does require time, thought, and effort, but the payoff has eternal consequences that will surely be far-reaching. I believe that your children's future spiritual life will be positively impacted if you radically choose to give Jesus preeminence in your home at Christmastime and all throughout the entire year.

As I have emphatically relayed in the chapters of this book, I believe that children are being put at a spiritual disadvantage and being set up for future disappointment when Santa is portrayed as the gift-giver at Christmastime. In contrast, teaching children to look to Jesus for their gifts teaches them to depend on God and avoid idolatry, and as a byproduct, their faith will be stoked. Another benefit is that children are taught to be givers as they follow Jesus' example of giving.

As a parent, God has given you the ability to choose what you will expose your child to, and they will ultimately follow your lead. When you point them to Jesus, Christ is kept in Christmas and kids experience the excitement of receiving gifts and praising the Lord for them. The transition from Santa to Jesus, therefore, should not be too difficult as long as there is an alternative that is enjoyable and seen as producing the same results.

Finally, when Christians celebrate Jesus' birthday in a festive way, kids have fun, focus on Jesus, and become rooted and grounded in their faith. Positive memories surrounding the things of God will help them stay anchored.

Conclusion

The Bible says, "Train up a child in the way he should go, And when he is old he will not depart from it" (Proverbs 22:6).

Through the activities cited in this book, you can create memorable moments and traditions that your children can carry into adulthood and implement in their own homes with their children. The legacy can be carried on for many generations to follow, and the best part is that God is glorified, and Jesus is lifted up. The Holy Spirit is welcomed and exalted in the home where these activities are seriously prioritized during the Christmas holiday season. Implementing the suggestions I've offered will help you to reach the goal of having your child embrace the idea that Jesus IS the ONLY reason for the season.

I hope you will share what I have written with family, friends, coworkers, and pastors. I believe you can help to start a revolution that will be instrumental in keeping Christ in Christmas, front and center where He truly belongs. I pray that a new way of thinking about this topic will take root, grow, and flourish in the body of Christ. **May you have a very merry Christ-centered Christmas!** May your home be filled with joy and happiness that overflow as you and your family celebrate the birth of Jesus Christ. Amen.

NOTES

CHAPTER 1

1. "Saint Nicholas," *Biography.com*, A&E Networks Television, 10 Sept. 2019, http://www.biography.com/people/st-nicholas-204635#death-and-legacy, (accessed December 21, 2017).

2. Brian Handwerk, "St. Nicolas to Santa: The Surprising Origins of Mr. Claus," National Geographic, 20 Dec. 2013, http://news.nationalgeographic.com/news/2013/12/131219-santa-claus-origin-history-christmas-facts-st-nicholas, (accessed December 21. 2017).

3. "Saint Nicholas," http://www.biography.com/people/st-nicholas-204635#death-and-legacy.

4. Lee Krystek, "AKA Santa Claus." The Museum of UnNatural Mystery, 2003, http://www.unmuseum.org/santa.htm, (accessed January 11, 2018).

5. "Saint Nicholas," http://www.biography.com/people/st-nicholas-204635#death-and-legacy.

6. Krystek, http://www.unmuseum.org/santa.htm.

7. "Saint Nicholas," http://www.biography.com/people/st-nicholas-204635#death-and-legacy.

8. Krystek, http://www.unmuseum.org/santa.htm.

9. Handwerk, http://news.nationalgeographic.com/news/2013/12/131219-santa-claus-origin-history-christmas-facts-st-nicholas.

10. Krystek, http://www.unmuseum.org/santa.htm.

11. "Saint Nicholas," http://www.biography.com/people/st-nicholas-204635#death-and-legacy.

12. Krystek, http://www.unmuseum.org/santa.htm.

13. MaryAnn Diorio, Ph.D., "The War on Christmas," MaryAnn Diorio, 24 Dec. 2018, https://maryanndiorio.com/2018/12/24/the-war-on-christmas#comment-6516, (accessed January 3, 2018).

CHAPTER 2

1. MaryAnn Diorio, Ph.D., "The War on Christmas," MaryAnn Diorio, 24 Dec. 2018, https://maryanndiorio.com/2018/12/24/the-war-on-christmas#comment-6516, (accessed January 3, 2018).

2. MaryAnn Diorio, Ph.D., https://maryanndiorio.com/2018/12/24/the-war-on-christmas#comment-6516.

3. Lia Russell (Journalist and Mother), in discussion with the author, July 2019.

CHAPTER 3

1. Christine Bacon, Ph. D., *The Super Couple: A Formula for Extreme Happiness in Marriage* (Virginia Beach: Koehlerbooks, 2016), 133.

2. Bacon, 134-137.

CHAPTER 5

1. James Cooper, "Christmas Presents," Why Christmas? Nov. 2000, https://www.whychristmas.com/customs/presents.shtml, (accessed February 21, 2017).

CHAPTER 6

1. Becca, "Ways to Keep Christ in Christmas," The Dating Divas, n.d., https://www.thedatingdivas.com/12-ways-to-keep-christ-in-christmas, (accessed November 5, 2019).

2. Lauren Greutman, "Why My Kids Get Only 3 Gifts During Christmas," Lauren Greutman, 15 Nov. 2016, https://www.laurengreutman.com/why-my-kids-get-only-3-gifts-during-christmas, (accessed October 30, 2019).

3. Becca, https://www.thedatingdivas.com/12-ways-to-keep-christ-in-christmas.

4. Becca, https://www.thedatingdivas.com/12-ways-to-keep-christ-in-christmas.

Jesus

IS the ONLY

reason for

the Season!

ABOUT THE AUTHOR

Tracey L. Moore, M.A. (a.k.a. "The Purposeful Poet"™) was born in Newport News, Virginia and raised in Norfolk, Virginia. She received a Bachelor of Science degree in Industrial Engineering from Virginia Tech and worked for several years as an engineer for a major electronics company in the Baltimore area. However, she felt unfulfilled in her engineering career. Therefore, she decided to pursue a career helping people through counseling according to biblical principles and obtained a Master of Arts degree in Christian Counseling from Oral Roberts University.

Tracey worked for several years in various social work arenas such as battered women's and homeless shelters, and also worked as a housing counselor. She also taught high school math for a brief time and continued to move forward in her determination to find her life's calling as the Holy Spirit would lead.

Undaunted and determined to self-actualize, she did much soul searching and decided to leave the teaching profession when God presented a divine opportunity for her to work for the Navy as a financial educator. This was a perfect fit because it harmoniously married her math, Christian counseling and teaching backgrounds, and she was able to hone her craft for several years and become an Accredited Financial Counselor. After her tenure as a contractor for the Navy, she worked as a financial counselor at a major credit union until God orchestrated her departure so that she could pursue her dream of becoming a poet, author, and speaker. She currently lives in Norfolk, Virginia.

Connect with Tracey

Website:
http://www.TraceyLMoore.com
Facebook:
http://www.facebook.com/TraceyLMoore2012
Twitter:
@TraceyLMoore1
YouTube:
https://www.youtube.com/channel/
UC-0A2_Ail4LICVkj3NHeAVA

****

If this book has been a blessing to you, will you please consider posting a review on Amazon.com and tell others about what you have read? Thanks so much!

If you enjoyed this book, you may also enjoy Tracey's first book, *Oasis for My Soul: Poems and Inspirational Writings for Spiritual and Personal Growth, Volume One.* To get your copy, please visit Amazon.com.

GOD WANTS TO QUENCH YOUR SPIRITUAL THIRST.

- Do you ever feel spiritually "dry"?
- Do you want a deeper, more personal relationship with God?
- Do you want to be emotionally whole?

Oasis for My Soul is a collection of poems, poetic prayers, praise and scripturally based inspirational writings intended to feed your spirit and refresh your soul. If you are having a spiritual "dry spell," the power-packed entries will hydrate, nourish, encourage, and inspire you to develop a deeper and more satisfying relationship with the Master, the true Oasis for our souls. You will be challenged to move to a higher plane in your walk with Christ through the writings, thought-provoking journaling exercises, and pertinent prayers that will help you to:

- Receive a brand new level of spiritual discernment and awareness.
- Enhance your personal and spiritual growth in the Lord.
- Build self-esteem and aggressively move toward wholeness.
- Maintain faith and hope during very difficult times.
- Challenge the devil's negative "thought bombs."

**FREE SCRIPTURE PRODUCTS
FROM THE PURPOSEFUL POET**

Please visit https://traceylmoore.com/store-2

**DIVINE DELIVERANCE
Deliverance Scriptures to Fuel Your Faith
King James Version
(MP3 RECORDING, 7 minutes)**

Have you been in a difficult situation for a very long time? Have you been asking God for deliverance? This MP3 recording is filled with deliverance scriptures (read by Tracey L. Moore) that will help you maintain your faith and believe God's power is on the way. The recording also includes the soothing, relaxing background nature sound of a babbling brook and can be coupled with the deliverance scriptures e-book Divine Deliverance for maximum spiritual impact. As you listen to the scriptures and read along with the recording, you will be encouraged to hold on to your faith in the midst of your trials.

DIVINE DELIVERANCE
Deliverance Scriptures to Fuel Your Faith
King James Version
(E-BOOK)

God is indeed a deliverer, and He is faithful to His Word. This e-book is filled with deliverance scriptures to fuel your faith and help you to hang on until you see victory. An inspirational quote and a poem ("Divine Deliverance") by Tracey L. Moore are included. This is a great companion to the deliverance scriptures MP3 recording with the same title. As you listen to the scriptures and read along with the recording, you will be encouraged to hold on to your faith in the midst of your trials.

WALK BY FAITH, NOT BY SIGHT
Faith Scriptures for Difficult Times
King James Version
(E-BOOK)

"Faith cometh by hearing, and hearing by the word of God" (Romans 10:17). This e-book is filled with faith scriptures that will help you to develop your faith "muscles" when you read and meditate on the verses over and over again. An inspirational quote and a poem ("Walk by Faith, Not by Sight") by Tracey L. Moore are included. When you read the Word of God regularly, you will be empowered by the Holy Spirit to believe God for the miraculous.

GOD IS YOUR HEALER
The Promises of God for Those in Need of Healing
King James Version
(E-BOOK)

Are you fighting an illness? God is still in the healing business! This e-book contains the healing promises of God for His children. Meditating on healing scriptures is like taking spiritual medicine, and what God's Word says about healing has been conveniently compiled in this e-book just for you. An inspirational quote and a poem ("God is Your Healer") by Tracey L. Moore are included. As you read the healing scriptures and meditate on the Word of God, you will be encouraged to stand in faith and believe God for your healing until you see results.

THE GIFT OF ENCOURAGEMENT
Scriptures of Encouragement for All Seasons
King James Version
(E-BOOK)

We all need a little encouragement sometimes. This e-book contains scriptures that will encourage you in good and bad times. As you read and meditate on the Word, you will be encouraged to hang in there and fight the good fight of faith, and you will be able to use these same verses to encourage others. A poem ("The Gift of Encouragement") and an inspirational quote by Tracey L. Moore are included. As you read the scriptures, your spirit will be encouraged. God's Word will help you gain the spiritual strength needed to continue to stand your ground on your own spiritual battlefield until you ultimately triumph over the enemy.

PEACE, BE STILL!
Peace Scriptures to Soothe the Anxious Soul
King James Version
(E-BOOK)

The Apostle Paul tells us in Philippians 4:6 to be anxious for nothing. Therefore, a peaceful state should be pursued by every believer, and this e-book contains scriptures that will help you to hold on to your peace. An inspirational quote and poem ("Peace") by Tracey L. Moore are included. As you meditate on these verses, the Word you receive will help to cultivate the fruit of the Spirit of peace in your life. This is a great companion to the peace scriptures MP3 recording with the same title. Please subscribe to the email list at www.TraceyLMoore.com to obtain a free MP3 download of *Peace, Be Still!*

FREE BONUS GIFTS
You are a valued reader!
Please go to
http://www.traceylmoore.com/ tlm/bonus_gifts.html
to download your free gifts!

Gift 1:

You will receive a free MP3 download entitled "Please Heal My Soul." This includes a collection of 5 poetry readings by Tracey (a.k.a. The Purposeful Poet™).

Gift 2:

You will receive a free download of personal affirmations with supporting scriptures to confess over your life daily. These affirmations are designed to help you renew your mind and develop a vision for your life.

MAY GOD BLESS AND PROSPER YOU!